DAY 1

- THINK -

Every year in sports, a new national champion is crowned. In baseball, it's the World Series; in football, the Super Bowl. When teams perform well, they gain more fans. The most popular athletes' jerseys from the winning teams sell at an incredible rate.

In music, each week a new artist tops the chart, clothing stores rise and fall in popularity and we actively watch certain television shows only to have them replaced by others. Over a lifetime we will follow hundreds of different sports, shows, artists, hobbies, and styles. If we were truly honest with ourselves, most of us would realize that we are bandwagon fans of hundreds of things. We follow because we feel like winners, we get recognition, we want to be trendy, and we want to fit in. Everyday we make a choice of who or what we will follow.

- FOCUS -

Read John 1:35-51. As you read, write down the names of everyone mentioned in this passage and who they were following at this point.

_____

_____

_____

Not unlike today, Jewish boys in the first century had aspirations of what they hoped to become. But instead of wanting to be a superstar athlete or an incredible businessman, the desire would have been to be a religious leader. Teachers of the Law and Rabbis were highly viewed in ancient Jewish culture. By the age of 13, the brighter boys would have been students or disciples of a Rabbi (Teacher). The other boys were sent off to work a trade like shepherding, farming, or fishing.

John the Baptist was a teacher who had attracted quite a crowd and came about from non-traditional methods. He simply began preaching a message of repentance. Because he didn't go through the traditional route of formal training in the synagogue, he attracted non-typical disciples who hoped that maybe they would somehow be able to become a Rabbi by non-traditional methods. So when Jesus comes along and John calls him the "Lamb of God", they thought their chances of being great would be better by following Jesus, instead of John. Jesus was open to their questions about who He was. He responded to them by saying, "Come and you will see."

- CONSIDER -

This same invitation to "come and see," is later given from Nathanael to his brother Phillip. Today, this same invitation is being offered to you. Over the next 30 days you will be given an invitation to "come and see" Jesus. You will be able to see if Jesus is worthy of your fandom, and more importantly, your devotion to follow Him completely.

There is no way the disciples had any idea what they were walking into when they walked away from John the Baptist and began following Jesus. It's probable that many of you are in the very same spot these disciples were in. Are you unsatisfied with where you are in life? Do you long for something more or to be more significant? Do you wish people looked at you as if you were more important than you really are? Almost everyone would say "yes" to these things.   We might even be willing to try anything in order to be satisfied, significant, and important. Jesus understands this and invites you to check Him out. However, consider yourself warned: He will do all of these things for you, but He will also redefine what everything means.

- APPLY -

Each day you'll be given a little something to chew on throughout the day. This may look like a challenge. It may be a conversation with someone. It may be prayer, or it may be an action. The desire is for you to not just read this and say, "oh that was nice," but to really wrestle with who Jesus is and let what you know about Him change the way you live.

Today, your mission is pretty simple. Throughout the day pay attention to all the things that take up your time. Ask yourself from time to time during the day: "Is this what I was created for?" Start off with a simple prayer asking God to reveal who Jesus is and how you could begin to follow Him.

EVENING

- REFLECT -

Write down in two sentences how you spent the day. Would you be fulfilled if you spent every day this way?

_____

_____

_____

Make a list of all the things you follow, from sports teams to clothing, etc.

_____

_____

_____

What are some of the significant changes you see in what you follow today and what you followed a year ago?

_____

_____

_____

What do you follow today that won't matter in 1, 5, and 10 years?

_____

_____

_____

Sometime tonight, ask God to open your eyes to see who Jesus is over the next 30 days.

DAY 2

- THINK -

One day, a high school student walked into class and noticed that the girl who sat at the desk next to him (that was also 9 months pregnant) was missing. Curiosity got the best of him, so he asked her friend where she was. She responded, "She had her baby last night." For some reason he felt obligated to go visit the girl in the hospital. They weren't really friends, and he felt a little awkward about showing up unannounced at the hospital to visit a girl who didn't have the best reputation.

He walked into the cold hospital room, and noticed that there were no flowers or cards…just a teenage girl watching television with her baby. The girl looked at him and asked, "What are you doing here?" He awkwardly responded, "I heard you had a baby so I thought I would come visit you." Dead silence filled the air as she stared in shock. Not knowing what to say next, he asked, "How are you doing?" She said, "Great, but I wish I had some McDonalds." Wanting to get out of the awkward conversation, he gladly volunteered to go get her some.

When he returned to the room, the girl said, "I really didn't think you would come back." She opened the sack and immediately began eating the fries like candy and looked up and asked, "Why are you so nice?"

At some point in your life you will most likely encounter a teenage girl who is pregnant. Teenage pregnancy is probably one of the most publicly shameful circumstances in the life of a teenager. The girl who is pregnant feels guilt and shame for what she has done, and the eyes of most peers look upon her with judgment. This is not just the reaction of the moral upright or Christians, but all of society. Usually the girl will remove herself from most activities and social places during her pregnancy because of the shame she feels.

- FOCUS -

Read John 4:1-26, and as you read, underline any new discovery about Jesus you see in the text.

The story of the teenage girl is very similar to the story we read in John 4. This woman was an outcast from society. She had a terrible reputation and was easily taken advantage of by men. We know this because it says she had five husbands and the man she was currently living with was not her husband. It makes sense why she would get water from the well during the hottest part of the day. She most likely wasn't welcomed nor did she want to get water with the other ladies from the town in the cool of the morning.

On this day she makes a surprising discovery when she encounters Jesus. She was a Samaritan, and most Jews did not associate with Samaritans. Samaritans were not even allowed to worship God in the temple. In addition, she was a female; and men did not speak with women in public besides their wives. Yet on this day, Jesus talks to her, and she discovers that He is the Messiah. This is the first time Jesus had shared with anyone that He was the one that the Old Testament referred to, that He was the Savior. And he chose to do so to a Samaritan, a woman, who was living in sin, who had the wrong impression about God, and was rejected by society.

- CONSIDER -

This is probably not the Jesus you have always heard about,
or at least who Christians often portray. Yet Jesus is willing to
destroy every barrier that would separate you from God. Gen-
der, race, reputation, mistakes, financial situation, and misguid-
ed beliefs will not stand in the way of Jesus wanting to reveal
himself to you. He wants to know you. He is so much greater
than what you have heard, and when He does reveal Himself
to you through His word, you too will be surprised by what you
discover about Him.

- APPLY -

As you go through the day today, intentionally have conversations with two different people. Choose one person who you
know is a Christian, and ask them why it is easy for them to
believe in Jesus. Then find another person who is not a believer
and ask them what barriers stand in the way of them believing in
Jesus.

Some may say the reason they believe in Jesus is because of
their parents, or because it makes sense, or because they know
they need forgiveness of their sin…they may even give you
evidence for Jesus' existence. On the other hand those who
don't believe might say it sounds like a fairytale, the miracles
are too hard to believe, but many will say something in regard
to the world they live in being too evil, Christians treating them
poorly or that there seems to be too many rules to follow to be a
Christian.

Is it possible that Jesus has a surprising discovery for both?

- REFLECT -

What are some the barriers standing between you and Jesus?

_____

_____

_____

What makes you think you have to overcome these barriers?

_____

_____

_____

Read John 4:27-42. What results do you see from this woman's discovery of Jesus?

_____

_____

_____

How does this woman saying "He told me everything I ever did" make you feel? Do you want Jesus to know you like this?

_____

_____

_____

Tonight ask Jesus to reveal Himself to you. This may be in His word, in another person, or in creation.

DAY 3

- THINK -

Have you ever noticed that are people who seem to love drama? It just seems to follow them everywhere they go. Yes, they complain about it all the time as if they "hate drama", but it's constantly around them. It doesn't take long to realize they are the source of the drama. These people are labeled "drama queens" (or kings). The reason they are dramatic is because it is a way to receive sympathy and attention. There is actually a mental disorder labeled "Histrionic personality disorder." This is well beyond the normal teenage drama, but if a teenager has an overwhelming desire to be noticed and receive attention through dramatic behavior, it could very well result in this disorder.

It may seem crazy that someone would want attention and sympathy so intensely that they would live a life of drama in order to receive their self-worth. Truth is they might actually hate drama, but have gotten addicted to being the center of attention.

- FOCUS -

Read John 5:1-15. Take a minute and write down your thoughts on this story.

_____

_____

_____

_____

Here is a man who had been an invalid for 38 years. He would hang out by a pool that was described as a place where, "an angel of the Lord would come down and stir up the waters. The first one into the pool after each such disturbance would be cured of whatever disease he had." This man was hoping to be healed, which makes us wonder why Jesus asked him if he wanted to "get well." Of course he did!

You can picture this man sitting by the pool, dramatically wanting sympathy and sounding like a three year-old in his whining response. "I would like to get better, but everyone else gets in first. I don't have anyone to help me. I'm too slow, I don't have friends, and people don't take turns." He was full of excuses and blamed everyone else for his problems.

- CONSIDER -

The tension sensed here is that this invalid wanted to tell his sob story, but didn't really want to get better. Why else would Jesus ask the question, "Do you want to get well?" That seems like a silly question to ask someone who has been unable to walk for 38 years. But this man had become quite comfortable with his life. He received attention, sympathy and always had an excuse for why he couldn't get better.

The tension may be the same for you. Most likely you can walk, but you have become quite comfortable with your paralyzing lifestyle and have no desire to change. It's even possible that you have quite a story. Parents divorced, abuse, low-income family, learning disability, or sexual identity issues might be part of your life. Jesus offers the healing of your heart, but this means you will have to change the way you live. You can't use the same excuses. You can't blame others. You have to let the drama go and remove yourself from the center of attention and put Jesus there. Excuses are a way to justify our wrongful actions. Do you want to get well?

Take a sheet of paper and write at the top, "Excuses Used."
Draw a line in the middle of the paper. As you go through the
day pay attention to how many excuses you hear or use. On
one side write down the excuse you used and on the other side
write down excuses you heard.

At the end of the day, under each excuse write down what
would be required of yourself or the other person if they did not
use an excuse.   Typically an excuse is used to place blame on
someone else, or avoid taking action over something you are
responsible for. Next to each excuse place a "B" for blaming
and an "A" for action.

EVENING

- REFLECT -

How many excuses did you hear today? What type of excuse
was used the most?

_____

_____   _____

_____

Why do you think people make so many excuses?

_____

_____

_____

What is in your life that you know needs to change? What is keeping you from changing? Could this just be an excuse?

_____

_____

_____

With this man who was an invalid, do you think his life became easier or more difficult after he was healed? Why?

_____

_____

_____

Is it possible that you are using an excuse to keep you from following Jesus?

_____

_____

_____

Spend a few moments asking God to reveal the things in your life you have used as excuses to keep from changing. It's possible you have become used to the drama of your circumstance and it has brought you attention, sympathy and self-worth. If this is you, then ask God to free you from your circumstances, because He wants to make you well.

DAY 4

MORNING

- THINK -

Expectations often have much to do with the way we feel about something. When you hear the hype all your friends are making about the best new movie, it impacts what you anticipate seeing. When you find out that your parents moved your annual family vacation from the sunny coastline to a regional motel, your shattered expectations generate a greater disappointment. When someone you thought you could trust betrays you, it hurts all the more deeply. Expectations can also play a role in your relationship with Jesus. If you're honest with yourself, you may begin to realize that your expectations of Jesus impact the way that you see and interact with him.

- FOCUS -

Start your day by reading Luke 23:8-12.

This event takes place toward the end of Jesus' life. He has already been betrayed by Judas, and has now been brought before Herod Antipas. Up to this point, Herod has been nothing more than a curious ear, catching bits and pieces about what Jesus has been doing. Excited to finally meet Jesus, he sets his heart on a front row seat to seeing Jesus perform a miracle. Not only does Jesus disappoint Herod by not doing a miracle, he also stays silent during Herod's batch of questions. Herod quickly makes a decision on how he feels about Jesus. Instead of becoming a fan or follower, he chooses to ridicule Jesus. Herod then plays dress up with Him before sending him off to another trial.

It's fairly obvious that Jesus did not meet Herod Antipas' expectations

Before you continue your day, take a moment to search your heart. What expectations do you have for Jesus? Is it possible that you have some standards that he has to meet for you in order for you to accept him as your Lord? Is your relationship with Jesus dependent on anything He must do in order to keep you happy?

One giant roadblock between many people and following Jesus is their own set of expectations. As you read scripture, it's evident that Jesus destroyed people's expectations. He had a clear sense of His calling, and people's expectations were not going to change the course He had set.

As you go about your day, consider whether you are willing to accept Jesus on his terms, and not yours. Jesus did not come to please you or bend to your wishes. He came to give you the opportunity to follow him, and following him means accepting him exactly the way He is.

Throughout the day, keep coming back to this question: are you willing to accept Jesus the way that He is? Pray about it. Saturate your mind with this thought.

EVENING

- REFLECT -

After weighing the decision throughout the day, are you willing
to come to Jesus on His terms?

What's your greatest challenge in accepting Jesus just as He is?

As you prayed today, what did you hear God speaking or reveal-
ing to you? What conclusion(s) did you come to?

Before falling asleep tonight, have an honest conversation
with God about this. Let him know your concerns, fears, decisions and what is going on in your heart.

D.T.R.

DEFINE THE RELATIONSHIP

IS YOUR RELATIONSHIP

WITH JESUS A 'CASUAL' ONE

OR IS IT 'EXCLUSIVE?'

DAY 5

- THINK -

One of the perks of being a spectator is the ability to watch casually with no expectations. If you're a fan of a sports team, everyone looks to see how passionate you are. Are you wearing team gear? Can you prove your worth in a battle of stats with a rival fan? Are you willing to paint your face to support your players? But as a spectator, you're off the hook. No one judges you for wearing neutral colors or being dispassionate after an impressive play. Of course, being a spectator also means that you forfeit any bragging rights or ownership in the game. In an election year, if you remain a spectator, you'll have no sway in who will be placed in office. If you remain a spectator when it comes to Jesus, you'll miss out on a transformational relationship that stretches from this lifetime through eternity.

- FOCUS -

Start your day by reading John 7:1-52. As you read, write down every statement where someone expresses an opinion about Jesus' identity.

During the third year of his ministry, Jesus has another opportunity to go to the Feast of Tabernacles (or Feast of Booths). This would have been one of three annual visits a Jewish male would have made to the temple in Jerusalem. Recognizing the hostility many of the Jews felt toward him, Jesus decides to arrive discreetly. Even before He makes His presence known, the crowds are murmuring about Him, wondering about His identity. This intensifies once Jesus begins to teach in the temple. Some spectators are asking questions. Others are ready to condemn Him. Opinions are running rampant, and nobody seems to have a firm handle on whom, exactly, Jesus is.

- CONSIDER -

Coming to an understanding of Jesus is essential to having a relationship with Him. Most likely, you've heard other people share their thoughts and opinions on Jesus. Maybe you have only learned things about Jesus from others up to this point. Perhaps you've let other people's thoughts about Jesus shape yours. It's even possible that you may have never even given consideration to Jesus' real identity. This can even be true if you have been in church your whole life!

There's no way to get beyond being a spectator of Jesus until you make up your mind about Him. And you can't make up your mind about him until you know Him. Of course, it isn't possible to know Him until you know about Him. This just makes sense, right?

- APPLY -

Today, you have one simple mission: figure out what you know about Jesus. This might be simple, or it might take some time. You may need to trace back where some of your thoughts on Him came from and weed out the opinions of others from the truth. There's a good chance that you'll want to pick up a Bible to investigate. Schedule some time today to think through this (it probably won't happen by chance). Don't be afraid to invite God into the conversation. Prayerfully ask for his help. He wants for you to know Jesus.

EVENING

What do you know about Jesus?

_____

_____

_____

Where have most of your thoughts and opinions on Jesus come from?

_____

_____

_____

What or who has influenced the way you feel about Jesus?

_____

_____

_____

Have you had any realizations about your relationship with Jesus?

_____

_____

_____

Take some time to think through what God has shown you so far through this journal. If appropriate, give God some thanks for what he's been doing in you.

DAY 6

- THINK -

D.T.R. These three letters can strike fear in the hearts of certain young men. What do they stand for? Define the relationship. It's the conversation in which a couple determines exactly where the level of commitment lies. Are we friends? Are we dating? A D.T.R. is when these questions get answers, and both parties say out loud what has been building in their hearts. Sometimes the D.T.R. can be awkward. Other times, it's a relief and exciting. No matter the kind, a D.T.R. is necessary to make sure that both parties are on the same page and know the level of commitment the other person has toward the relationship.

- FOCUS -

Start your day by reading Matthew 16:13-19.

It wasn't just the crowds at the Feast of the Tabernacles who were trying to figure out who Jesus was; His disciples were in the same position. Jesus unleashes the question, "Who do people say that I am?," to His followers. They blurt out a list of the trending opinions of various people. But Jesus isn't satisfied with this feedback. He makes the question personal. Jesus asks for their response to His identity. He wants to know what they're thinking about him. Peter is the one who responds. He bears his heart to Jesus and the disciples. He defines his relationship with Jesus.

- CONSIDER -

Knowing about Jesus isn't enough. If you stopped reading the journal at day 5, then you'd be missing out on a crucial truth: Jesus cares about the place He holds in our lives. Keeping tabs on other's opinions of Jesus doesn't cut it. What you think about Jesus matters, and so does the level of commitment you have toward Him.

- APPLY -

The rest of this journal is built around what you're about to tackle today. Now is the time for you to define your relationship with Jesus. What place does He hold in your life? How committed are you to a relationship with him? Are you a spectator, fan or follower?

Here are some thoughts that might help bring some clarity:

A **spectator** is an observer, someone who watches.
A **spectator** might say, "I'm just checking things out" when it comes to Jesus.

A **fan** is an enthusiastic admirer.
A **fan** could be caught saying something like, "Jesus is great. I like Him a lot."

A **follower** is one who denies himself, takes up his cross daily and follows Jesus.
A **follower** would say, "I will obediently follow Jesus no matter the cost."

Before you come to any conclusions, stop to pray and ask for God to reveal the truth to you. Ask for Him to keep you from being self-deceived or from remaining oblivious to reality. If you haven't set aside enough time to pray right now, take the first opportunity you get to have a conversation with God about this question. Maybe you'll have some time on the way to school, in study hall, on a break from work or in a lull between activities.

Whenever the opportunity arises, seize the opportunity to spend some time seeking His guidance.

After you've had time to pray, ask yourself where you're at right now. Are you a spectator? A fan? A follower? Give yourself the freedom to answer honestly without feeling bad about where you are. Re-read over the statements above. Which description sounds the most like you? Which statement could you most truthfully say? Let this be the thought you return to throughout the day. If it will help you, take this book along with you today to reference as you reflect.

EVENING

- REFLECT -

Which of the three categories do you fall into right now: spectator, fan, or follower?

_____

_____

_____

Are you content with where you currently are? Why or why not?

_____

_____

_____

What will it take for you to move toward where God is calling you to be?

_____

_____

_____

As you think about surrendering everything to follow Jesus, what is your greatest fear?

_____

_____

_____

As you wrap up your day today, imagine what it would be like to follow Jesus unconditionally. As you begin to see that picture come into focus, ask God to help that image to become a reality in your life.

DAY 7

- THINK -

Two rival high school basketball teams, which were separated by the Mississippi River, were playing each other in their annual game. The larger school was much more athletic and talented this particular year. They also had 600 or more students in attendance at their school. To call it a rivalry had very little to do with the score or the competition. During the second half of the game one of the players from the larger school stole the ball at center court. After dunking the ball in his team's basket, he ran back to the center of the court and bowed several times. He received a technical foul and the coach took him out of the game. While everything about the dunk was performed correctly, the showboating afterwards was wrong.

Most of the time, right is always right and wrong is always wrong. But scripture seems to indicate that there is a time when right is wrong.

- FOCUS -

Read Matthew 6:1-4.

Certainly Jesus does not have anything against people doing kind acts for other people. As a matter of fact, if you read through the New Testament you will see many times that we are encouraged to serve one another, to look out for the needs of others, or to put others ahead of ourselves. So it's not the righteous act that is wrong here, but the motivation behind he action.

Fans of Jesus love the applause of men. This is not a new concept; it has been around since sin entered the world. You see it with many of the men God chose to use in scripture, you see it in Jesus' disciples, and you see it among Christians today. Jesus opens the eyes of his audience by pointing out that even when our actions might be right, if the motivation is to show how good you are, then your heart is in the wrong place.

- CONSIDER -

As a child, your parents or teachers may have often encouraged you to share with others. At this age, the hope is that as you mature sharing would become part of who you are. However, if you only shared to get something in return, your righteous act would be overshadowed by your selfish motivation.

There are many fans of Jesus who model their life after many of the principles of Jesus, but it is not because they have a desire to be like Jesus, but because of the attention they receive. They walk around with their "holier than thou" attitude looking down on others and always talking about how they don't drink, use drugs, or have sex before marriage. They are sure to tell you about all the charitable things they do. These actions may be good, but if their motivation isn't love for Jesus, but self-promotion, then they are just fans of Jesus.

- APPLY -

Today's challenge is to help someone out by doing something anonymously. It may be an encouraging letter, it may be paying for someone to participate in an event, it may be cleaning up for your youth pastor after church, it could be anything…but do your best to make it something where no one else will know or see you do it.

This is not to be done so you can feel good about yourself. The temptation will be to tell others what you have done. Refrain from telling anyone. After all, the reward of men is momentary; but the reward from the father in heaven is eternal.

EVENING

- REFLECT -

What did you learn about your motivation today?

_____

_____

_____

Were you able to complete the challenge? Was it hard not to tell? Why is it so difficult?

_____

_____

_____

How could changing your motivation change the way you serve and give?

_____

_____

_____

What do you think non-believers think about those who self-promote their good deeds?

_____

_____

_____

Why is it important to remember the words, "Be Careful" at the beginning of Matthew 6:1?

_____

_____

_____

DAY 8

- THINK -

In every group of friends there is always one who talks the most. If you tell a story about driving in a car really fast, they have driven a car faster. If you have jumped off a 20-foot cliff, they have jumped off one higher. Their stories are always bigger and better than everyone else's. Most of the time their stories are so exaggerated everyone just writes them off as being fake.

Several years ago there was a woman who made the claim she was in one of the twin towers when the terrorists attacked on September 11th. Her story riveted reporters as she told details of her amazing escape. Her story was so amazing, people rallied around her to listen. Then several years later it was revealed that the story was a lie. We hear these stories and think, "How could someone use others in order to promote themselves?"

- FOCUS -

Read Matthew 6:5-13. Underline every place you see instruction on how to pray. Write what you think God was trying to communicate.

_____

_____

_____

Jesus is giving instructions to the crowd to correct some false assumptions on what a disciple of His should look like. This culture they were part of was a highly religious culture. Many of the people who had risen to power and authority in the community were men of religion. In an effort to draw attention to themselves and receive recognition from others, many of the religious leaders had taken on some pretty bad habits.

You could say these men were fans of God, but didn't want to pursue a relationship with him. They would stand on corners and pray these long elaborate prayers with big words that most people never use in a normal conversation. These prayers were not said as a way to communicate with God, but as a way of personal promotion. These prayers were said for the benefit of the onlookers, and to put themselves on a higher spiritual level.

- CONSIDER -

Imagine you go out on a date with your significant other. As you sit down at the table you begin to tell them how great they are. You compliment their outfit, tell them how nice their hair looks, etc. Now, let's pretend you are announcing this loudly for the whole restaurant to hear. And when it gets time to order, you shout, "Order anything you want, it's on me," as you look around the room for other patrons to be impressed by your actions.

Of course we would say this is awkward. Yet this is the type of thing being done here. God's desire is to have an intimate relationship with His people. Jesus sets the example and gives us insight into what an authentic relationship with God looks like. The point of the text is not to say it is wrong to pray in public, or to even have long prayers; but when the heart behind our praying is so others will think we are good Christians, then that falls short of what God desires.

- APPLY -

When you pause to pray be sure to check your motives. When you bow your head at lunch, are you really praying; or do you just want those around you to not look down upon you because you didn't pray before you took a bite?

If you pray out loud in front of others, avoid the temptation to impress others with big words and long prayers. Remember you are talking to your Father in Heaven who already knows what you are going to ask. He just longs to hear from you regardless of how impressive you sound.

Try to pray modeling the Lords Prayer:

- Start off by telling God how awesome He is.
- Then let Him know you will submit to His desires.
- Ask Him for the needs you have today.

EVENING

- REFLECT -

How did your prayer times with God change today?

_____

_____

_____

Do you ever find yourself using God to promote yourself? In what ways?

_____

_____

What part of the passage from earlier today made the biggest impact on you?

_____

_____

_____

How would believing that God already knows what you are going to ask make you feel about prayer?

_____

_____

_____

How would seeing God as a father change your prayer life?

_____

_____

_____

DAY 9

- THINK -

When it comes to fans, some have much more fun than others. There are fans who are captivated by every great feat, every point scored, and every aspect of the game. But then, there are other fans who tend to wind up miserable during the game. This kind of fan is the nail biter. He's the fan that forgets to breathe during the game. She's the fan that buries her face in her hands because she just can't bear to watch the outcome of the next play. The nail biter worries nonstop that his or her team will lose or that the other team will get ahead. Sometimes a winning team can still cause panic for the nail biter, who is freaked out by the potential possibility of loss later in the game. The nail biter experiences so much anxiety throughout the game that it's not even fun for him or her to watch. The nail biter needs a brown bag, an inhaler, and a strong friend to catch them when they're about to pass out. The nail biter is a nervous wreck.

- FOCUS -

Start your day by reading Matthew 6:25-34.

Just like the previous few fan case studies, this teaching comes straight from Jesus' mouth as part of a famous lesson that has come to be known as "The Sermon on the Mount." Here, Jesus unpacks an incredible about of truth for his would-be followers. After addressing several of the practices that should characterize his followers, he brings up the discussion of worry. Jesus reveals that worry has no place in the life of the believer. Through numerous rhetorical questions and simple analogies, he explains how the deep love of God translates into care for his people. As a result, His people need only to place their trust in Him, rather than giving themselves ulcers over potential problems or misplaced priorities. While this teaching could be interpreted as a sharp rebuke, Jesus words also offer freedom for those held captive by fear and worry. Instead, the people of God should begin by seeking first the Kingdom of God. God will take care of the rest.

- CONSIDER -

Chances are you've got some worries of your own. There is also a good likelihood that you have no idea how many things you worry about in a day. Everything from a concern over a nearly-formed pimple to a fear that you'll be a failure at life – it's all part of worry. So, what if you could see all the times that you worried in a day?

- APPLY -

Today, you're going to track all the things you worry about. This will probably take some concentration and a few supplies. Unless you have perfect recall memory, you'll need some way to record instances of worry. You may want to grab a pen and a journal, some scrap paper, or a portable electronic device. Each time you encounter something that you're worried about, write down (or type) specifically what it is. This may be a challenge or seem a little trivial, but give it your best effort.

After you've written down your worry, say a brief sentence prayer (eyes-open prayers are okay, by the way). For example, if you're worried about people staring at that zit, pray something like, "God, help me to find my value in being your child, and not in a perfect complexion." Remember what Jesus said in Matthew 6:33, and replace your worry by seeking after God's kingdom. Rather than getting anxious over whether you'll have friends to sit next to at lunch, ask God to lead you to the seat where you can have influence for Him. Instead of worrying about the fight your parents just had, pray for God to be in the center of their marriage. Allow each moment of worry today to become a cause to re-focus your eyes on Jesus.

EVENING

- REFLECT -

What do you think about the list of worries you tracked today?

_____

_____

_____

What was it like to begin taking your worry moments and turning them into prayer moments?

_____

_____

_____

If you continued to repeat this exercise every day, would it change your perspective? Your anxiety level?

_____

_____

_____

What did God teach you today?

If you had any moments of surrender or peace today as a result of your focus and prayer, thank God for his goodness and for honoring your obedience.

DAY 10

- THINK -

It's crazy how our culture has been captured by Idolism. No, I don't mean the worship of idols (although that may be true as well), but we have become enamored with talent shows similar to American Idol. It has received more consecutive number one watched seasons than any other program on television.

We watch contestants get up and perform. We hear their story, which often captures our heart, and then we listen to the judges either praise or criticize the contestant. When negative criticism is given to a performer that is a fan favorite you can hear the crowd boo-ing, especially if the criticism is too harsh.

What might be the most interesting part of the show is the point when the fans are able to be the judges and vote on who moves on and ultimately wins the title. Fans love the fact they don't have to make much of an investment in the show, but they get to participate in judging the contestants.

- FOCUS -

Read Matthew 7:1-6. Write down what caught your attention from this text.

"Don't judge me!" is one of the most popular sayings among people today. Sometimes this is said in the spirit of good humor, but most of the time it is said to someone who has been critical of another's lifestyle or behavior. Jesus was speaking to a large crowd that lived in a very critical, judgmental society. The religious leaders of the time were highly critical of people and put pressure on people to follow the rules. There was no concern about internal transformation, but external actions.

Jesus wanted the people to know it's not about judging the actions of man and beating them down for being unable to follow the rules, but it was about the transformation of the heart. It only takes a minimum investment to get someone to change their behavior, but takes an ongoing consistent relationship to change their heart. Jesus set the example in his interaction with sinners. He dealt with them in grace and truth. He did acknowledge their sin in order to call them to a life transforming relationship with Him.

- CONSIDER -

Fans of Jesus will take on many of the principles Jesus introduces. They cut certain things out of their life in order to look the part. Let's be honest, the moral laws established in scripture really are what is best for society. Who doesn't like people who are honest, trustworthy, faithful, peaceful, giving, kind and merciful…just to name a few. No one likes it when people use dishonest gain, steal, or lie about others. However, if our Christianity is nothing more than following the rules, then we have the biggest skyscraper beam hanging out our eye socket. The picture Jesus uses is ridiculous. The fan of Jesus points out the sawdust in the eye of someone who hasn't got the rules mastered, and doesn't even realize following the rules as a substitute for heart transformation is the bigger problem.

To give this some real legs think of a couple that chooses to date each other. Let's say the guy is completely in love with the girl. He serves her faithfully and does everything she could ever want, not because he has to, but out of the overflow of his love for her. The girl on the other hand follows all the rules because she likes the idea of dating and loves the fact she can say she has a boyfriend and her Facebook status can say "In a Relationship." But she does not love the guy and every day feels like it is a task for her.

Essentially the girl is just playing a role. This is the biblical definition of a hypocrite, someone who is just playing a role like an actor in a theatre. But it is not who they really are. Jesus makes it clear that just playing the part of a true follower is a big problem.

- APPLY -

We all at times feel like fans of Jesus. We all are quick to identify other fans as well. When we see another fan of Jesus we often compliment their fan gear, but rarely do we pay attention to how Christ is transforming their life. We think they can pray really well, they give lots of money, they are at every event, and they are close with the youth minister or pastor and their family all goes to church. Today I want you to take the plank out of your own eye and look beyond the surface to the heart of a person.

EVENING

- REFLECT -

What bothered you the most about today's passage?

_____

_____

_____

Who do you find yourself most like: the one looking down on others or the one looked down upon? Why?

_____

_____

_____

Why do you think so many people call Christians "hypocrites"?

_____

_____

_____

What is the plank or beam hanging out of your eye that needs to be removed so you can lovingly help others?

_____

_____

_____

DAY 11

MORNING

- THINK -

There is an art to selecting a quality pick up basketball team. You look around and see who has the most gear on. If they look athletic, have nice shoes, headband, wristbands, shooting sleeve, calf sleeve, authentic team uniform, and name brand bag, you should steer clear of choosing those guys. They are called "Posers." They look the part and it's tempting to want them on the team, but often you will be disappointed by their actual abilities.

There are Christian "Posers" as well. A youth pastor told the story about a group of boys from his church called the "Suit Crew." Every Sunday they would show up to church dressed in their Sunday best. They had their suits on, Bible in hand, hair done and walked around like they were the best of Christians. Parents would see these young men all dressed up. They would be respectful as they passed church leaders and parents replying with "Yes Ma'am" and "Yes Sir." Then the youth service would begin and they would sit in the back talking, making fun of others, looking down on those who had less, and influencing the younger students to do the same. At the Christian school they attended they were known as troublemakers as well, but they were very good at hiding who they really were. Many students were hurt by them and often said, "I can't believe Christians would act like that."

Read Matthew 7:15-23. What does this passage say about consistency?

_____

_____

_____

Apparently even in Jesus time there were people who would take God's word and twist it and manipulate it to fit their lifestyle. They would come across with smooth cunning words that would make you feel good about the life you are living, but did not mean anything they said was true. Jesus said they are like a wolves dressed in sheep's clothing. If you have ever watched Animal Planet you know that there are certain animals you never put together. Well, you can put them together and it makes for an exciting chase, but one party always ends up getting eaten. A wolf among sheep is disastrous.

Not everyone who calls themselves "Christian" are really followers of Jesus. In first century culture there were many men who called themselves prophets of God. They would mimic the actions of the other true prophets, but their message was false. They were fans of God because of the benefits of having a crowd follow them, but their message was not from God. In the same way there are many people today who are fans of Jesus, but distort His Word to fit their lifestyle and to get innocent sheep to follow them.

So the question is "how do you tell fan from a follower? How do you tell an authentic from a fake? How do you tell a sheep from a wolf, dressed in sheep's clothes?"

We could easily say it's by the size of their Bible, or how many times they attend church a week, or the group of friends they hang around, how many scriptures they can quote, if they only listen to Christian music, if they have been on a mission trip, or how much money they put in offering. Yet as good as all of these things may be, this is not what Jesus says we should use as a measurement of someone who is a follower. Fans can do all of these things and they can do them well. Fans often pose as followers, but fall short in one major area. Jesus says He will know true followers by their fruit. Many who pose as followers will get the most frightening words in all of scripture, "I never knew you. Away from me, you evildoers!"

- APPLY -

Following Jesus means that areas of your life must change. Far too often we hear people say, "Yes I am a Christian, but that doesn't mean I have to change." Fans of Jesus really admire His life and what He did, but do not want it to affect their life. Wolves often try to justify their actions and make them sound as if they are acceptable to Jesus. If the person you follow always says what you want to hear, then it's likely they are not speaking truth. So today the application is a heightened awareness of those around you. Look at the character of who they are and not the outward appearance.

- REFLECT -

What are some areas or places in life where you have been a "Poser"?

_____

_____

_____

Since you have started following Jesus what areas of your life have changed the most?

_____

_____

_____

Much of what Jesus speaks of in regards to "Fans" has to do with external practices. What are some practices people value, but mean little to Jesus? What do you see from scripture that Jesus is most concerned about?

_____

_____

_____

Today were there any warning signs you noticed? What were they?

_____

_____

DAY 12

MORNING

- STOP -

Before going any further, pause to prepare your heart for today's journal page. Block out everything that's trying to bombard you or overtake your focus. Take a deep breath and start the day with prayer. Invite God into your day, your heart, this moment. When you're ready, then move ahead.

- THINK -

When traveling from Cincinnati, Ohio, to Louisville, Kentucky, you take I-71 South.   It's the fastest, most direct route between the two cities. The journey is typically smooth and easy. However, there's one major thing that you cannot miss for this to work. Interstates 71 and 75 overlap for several miles when heading south from Cincinnati. The only way to make it from Cincinnati to Louisville is to exit onto the off-ramp from I-75 onto I-71. Interstate 75 is wide and inviting. Interstate 71's exit ramp is narrow and has a small window of access. Much of the traffic just keeps heading south at the juncture. If a person is driving down this stretch, it's incredibly easy to miss the off ramp. If one happens to miss the exit and continues ahead, he or she will end up in Lexington. Lexington is just a little more than an hour's drive from Louisville. By missing out on this one pivotal decision point, a driver can easily wind up 76 miles off course!

- FOCUS -

Start your day by reading Matthew 7:13-14.

Sometimes what looks like the right way isn't actually the right way. Jesus offers a simple picture: a big, wide road and a small, narrow road. The wide road is large and inviting. This road is well-traveled. The narrow road is small, cramped, unpopulated. The natural assumption would be that the wide road would be safe and lead to the desired destination, but Jesus flips expectation on its head. He explains that the narrow road is life-giving, while the wide road leads only to destruction. What appears to be right to most of the people is actually wrong.

- CONSIDER -

The implications of Jesus' teaching are far-reaching. Jesus fails to readily identify who are the many and the few. It might be easy to infer that He's talking about believers versus non-believers. But Jesus doesn't say that. One might assume that Jesus is championing the Jews and condemning the pagans, but this passage doesn't teach that. You might breathe a sigh of relief for the people you go to church with, but no one is expressly given a free pass here.

What Jesus reveals in this passage is that the narrow road is lonely. The narrow road deviates from the crowd, whomever they may be. The narrow road can only be reached through the narrow gate, and it just might be easy to overlook.

Jesus' initial invitation to those around Him was "Come and see." Later on, this invitation becomes, "Come, follow me." Make no mistake, Jesus' invitation to come and follow Him has a cost. Following Jesus means choosing the narrow road. Following Jesus means taking the off ramp from status quo to full surrender. Following Jesus doesn't happen by accident: it's a conscious choice.

- APPLY -

Simply visualize the wide and narrow roads today. Think
through the perks and costs of each. Imagine where you are.
Consider where you want to be. Weigh out the price of taking the ramp onto the narrow road. As you meditate and pray
through this thought, examine your heart to see if you're ready
to lay it all down to follow the narrow road. Remember, you
don't end up on the narrow road by accident; it's a very intentional choice.

EVENING

- REFLECT -

When you picture the wide and narrow roads, what images
come to mind? What do they represent?

_____

_____

_____

How difficult do you think it is to get onto the narrow road? To
stay on it?

_____

_____

_____

Knowing that exiting onto the narrow road will come at a price, are you willing to do what it takes to go there?

_____

_____

_____

Before ending your day, consider whether you're ready to move on to the narrow road. If you are, pray and ask God to help you to get on and stay on the narrow road. As you pray, visualize yourself moving away from the mainstream traffic and toward Jesus on the narrow road.

DAY 13

- THINK -

Every year around the first of the year you will see hundreds of people flooding to fitness centers in an effort to accomplish their new year's resolution. They head to health food stores, buy pills, protein, and workout magazines. For weeks they will hit the weight room and run on cardio machines, but after a while with no results many will walk away frustrated because they saw no results just wishing there was a magic pill.

This was the case with one man who was going to begin training in January to get that beach body he desired. After a few weeks of training he vocalized his frustration of not getting any leaner. Then another student who happened to be at the gym at the same time as him took of photo of the guy on an elliptical machine drinking a Venti (large) Starbucks Frappuccino. In order to get desired results you have to deny yourself a few things and change your lifestyle.

- FOCUS -

Read Luke 9:23-27. Write down vs. 23 as a definition of a follower of Jesus.

_____

_____

_____

A fan of Jesus will try to accept the invitation to follow Jesus, but they don't want to say no to themselves. Yet this is not at all what it means to deny himself. To deny yourself is more than just saying no to yourself or resisting something. The idea is that you do not even acknowledge or recognize your own existence.

Read Luke 9:57-62. Jesus makes it clean that a true follower of Him will deny himself in three major areas.

"Foxes have dens and birds have nests, but the Son of Man has no place to lay his head." What Jesus is saying here is we have to Deny our Comforts

This man says the right thing to Jesus. He says I will go wherever you want me to go. Jesus points out that he will not have all he comforts he had become accustomed to. It's difficult for us to deny ourselves in a world that says it's all about you.

"Let the dead bury their own dead." Jesus was saying that those who want to follow Him must Deny what we Cherish.

This man said he would follow Jesus, but first he had to take care of those things that meant a lot to him. Family in this culture was extremely important. To leave your family early would run the risk of losing some or all of your inheritance. To ask for your inheritance early was to tell your family they are dead to you.

We have our sacred cows or things we cherish as well. Education, cars, family business, vacations, health, and safety are just a few. None of these are bad, but when they stand in the way of us living in denial they can be destructive.

"No one who puts a hand to the plow and looks back is fit for service in the kingdom of God." This man wanted to follow on His own terms, but Jesus says followers must Deny our Conveniences.

Some of the responses by Jesus sound harsh. To this last guy
He says, "you are either in or you are out." You have to make a
choice to follow Jesus all the time in every area of your life, not
just when it is convenient.

- CONSIDER -

When you agree to deny yourself and follow Jesus you are saying, "I choose Jesus over my friends. I choose Jesus over my
education. I choose Jesus over my wardrobe. I choose Jesus
over my dating life. I choose Jesus over my family. I choose
Jesus over money. I choose Jesus over the expectations others have placed on my life. I choose Jesus over popularity. I
choose Jesus over my freedoms. I choose Jesus over porn. I
choose Jesus over getting even. I choose Jesus."

This might sound like following Jesus is choosing a life of mis-
ery. If your heart is set on all of those other things and you love
them more than Jesus, then you will be miserable. However,
you will not find a person who has given their heart completely
to someone complain about having to sacrifice for them. Committed love is best demonstrated through sacrifice.

- APPLY -

Take a minute and write down all the things in your life you
might have to say "no" to in order to follow Jesus completely.
Don't just put down the obvious things like party scene, drugs,
or sex although those may make the list, but write down the
every day things you know are difficult for you to sacrifice.

Then keep this note posted somewhere for a few days adding,
to it when you come across something else. Then when you are
ready to deny yourself the items on the list, take it out and burn

it. This is a sign you are ridding them permanently from your life.

EVENING

- REFLECT -

What hesitations do you have when it comes to following Jesus?

_____

_____

_____

Which of the three people in Luke 9:57-62 do you most identify with? Why?

_____

_____

_____

Create your own "I choose Jesus over…" list.

_____

_____

_____

Were you able to burn your list of things you are going to say "no" to? What will be the most difficult thing to deny yourself of?

_____

_____

DAY 14

- THINK -

Most of us can remember playing follow the leader as a kid. We would walk down the sidewalk, jump over a puddle, walk across a balance beam, hop on one leg, or follow some sort of facial expression. It was always a fun game as a kid, especially when you were the leader.

Imagine playing this same game with Jesus the last week of His life. He was wrongly accused, but remained silent. He was mocked, but did not return insults. He was beaten with a whip, which would have exposed His internal organs and bones, but He did not try to escape. Then He was nailed to a cross and only offered forgiveness. That's a tough example to follow.

- FOCUS -

Read Luke 9:23-27. Underline this passage in your Bible and then circle the words "Deny," "take up cross," and "follow"

Read Philippians 2:5-11

Fortunately for us the text says your "attitude" should be the same as that of Christ Jesus. As a follower of Jesus we do not have to make it our life ambition to literally live like Jesus. The meaning of following Jesus is not wearing a white robe, walking the same roads in Israel, and trading your car for a donkey. It does not mean we go out looking to be beaten, mocked and hung on a cross, but it does mean we have to be willing to live this sort of life. Fans admire what Jesus did for them, but followers are willing to walk the same path and take on the same attitude as Jesus. This is what Jesus meant when He said, "take up your cross, daily."

The cross was a symbol of humility. Crucifixion was the cruelest form of punishment. The idea was to make a statement to the crowd that this person was powerless and a nothing. It was to publicly humiliate the person who was being crucified.

The cross was a symbol of Suffering. Roman soldiers often beat the criminals prior to crucifixion. A large percentage never made it through normal flogging, which the Hebrew law limited to 40 lashes, but the Roman law had no restrictions except that the person must have enough strength to carry a cross. The criminal would then have to carry the horizontal beam of the cross they were going to hang on to the place of death.

The cross was a symbol of death. Nobody who hung on the cross lived. The idea was for them to die a slow, painful death. As they hung on the cross the onlookers would see the person hanging and it would discourage others from following the person's example or you would receive similar punishment.

- CONSIDER -

If you want to be a follower of Jesus you have to take up your cross daily. This means you have to have an attitude of humility. Humility isn't depriving yourself of everything good, but an intentional lowering. It's seeing others as better than yourself.

Taking up your cross means you have to be willing to suffer. We see all throughout Jesus' life He suffered. True followers will suffer for Christ. If you have never suffered for Christ you need to evaluate if you are really following Him. As a follower you do not look for suffering, but you do not run from it. The Bible says suffering is one of the main ways we identify with Christ.

Taking up your cross means you die to self. Deitrich Bonhoeffer said, "When Christ calls a man, He bids him to come and die." Most of us don't realize when we chose to follow Jesus and surrendered our lives to Him we died right then and there. You gave up your right to live as you want and told Christ to do with your life what He wants. "When you are dead you are no longer concerned about your life." (NAF pg. 166)

- APPLY -

Jesus indicates to us that taking up your cross is a choice we have to make every single day. It's not a once and done type of scenario, but each morning we make a decision to follow Christ's example.

Today we want you to ask three people these simple questions.

1. What are you willing to die for?
2. What characteristics in a person do you admire the most?
3. What lessons do you learn from suffering?

Read Philippians 2:1-11 from the Message version

EVENING

- REFLECT -

What is the hardest part of taking up your cross?

_____

_____

_____

What does dying to self look like in your life?

_____

_____

_____

Read through Philippians 2:5-11 and write down all the ways
Jesus humbled himself.

_____

_____

_____

What did you learn from asking the questions in the application?

_____

_____

_____

DAY 15

- THINK -

We have all been asked to do something that doesn't make sense. This is different than doing something crazy or stupid that would cause you to break your neck or go to jail. We are talking about something that is very doable, but goes against all better judgment. Doing something that doesn't make sense would be writing down a list of all the possible solutions to a problem, then choosing the one that makes little sense.

In 2006 Jason McElwain, a high school senior who had autism, was the team manager for Greece Athena High School basketball team. The last game of the season the coach of the team decided to put Jason in a uniform and put him in the game. When their team was winning by a sizeable amount with four minutes left Jason was put into the game. The next four minutes would be talked about for months. Jason made six three pointers and scored 20 pts.

This was a performance from a boy who was considered too small to make the junior varsity team, who lacked social skills of normal kids, who didn't even talk until he was five. However, he was dedicated to the team, took on the manager (water boy) job and showed up to every practice watching and shooting around. Did it make sense? Did anyone expect him to play? Did anyone think he would actually score in the game?

- FOCUS -

Read Luke 9:23-27. Commit this passage to memory today

Read Luke 5:1-11

If you were to look at this passage chronologically you would find these men who were fishing with Jesus had actually traveled with him for a small period of time. In fact, in John chapter one Jesus told Peter to follow him before, so this was Peter's second call to follow. We don't really know for sure why Peter went back home and went back to his old life of fishing, but we can make some assumptions from scripture.

We see from Luke 4:38 that his mother-in-law was sick. So pressure from his wife to be home and take care of matters was there. Fishing was Peter's job and source of income and after traveling with Jesus for a few weeks, money was probably getting a little tight. So the pressure was on for Peter and the crew to catch some fish, which is why Peter would have been fishing rather than hanging out with Jesus. He had priorities he had to take care of.

Luke 5 tells us Peter had been fishing all night long, but hadn't caught any fish. So the mood is not pleasant and the clean up miserable. This is when Jesus asks them to put their boats out a ways from shore so he could fish. After speaking to the crowd Jesus then asks Peter to put out into deep water, and let down the nets for a catch.

This does not make sense. Fishing with a net is only effective in shallow waters and fish only come to the shallows at night. Jesus, the non-fisherman, tells Peter to put out into deep water during the middle of the day to catch fish. When they did this they caught so many fish the nets began to break. At this point Peter falls with his face to the fish and ask Jesus "go away from me for I am a sinful man." Jesus responds by telling Peter "Follow me, and I will make you fishers of men."

Peter clearly felt guilty because he doubted Jesus. He doubted Jesus could help him catch fish, he doubted Jesus could provide for his needs, he doubted Jesus could use someone like him. Jesus assures Peter by letting Peter know that he would be on the one to reshape Peter's life, but what he needed to do was follow.

Is it possible you are having one of those moments as well? Are you at a place where following Jesus doesn't make a lot of sense? Following Jesus might mean you walk away from a relationship. Following Jesus might mean you say no to a scholarship and yes to ministry. Following Jesus could mean changing your family's religious tradition. Following Jesus could mean forgiving someone who wronged you. Following Jesus could mean changing your lifestyle in order to reach a different group of people. The question comes down to whether or not you trust Jesus enough to follow. If you do, He promises to "make you" into what He desires.

- APPLY -

Take 30 minutes today and go to a location where you are able to watch many people. Write down as many similarities you can find between people. It could be their actions, clothing, hairstyle, or shopping preferences. Then ask yourself, "Who are they following?"

What we find in this world is although there are many styles; there are very few originators. Yes, many people want to have their own style or flair, but often they mimic the style of someone else. Most of us are just the evolution of a style of the past. This is why people always encourage you to hang on to your old clothes because the style will come back. It usually does with a slightly different flair.

Now ask yourself whom you are following? Are you following parents, friends, the latest trend, or Jesus? Your external style may look slightly different than your parents and you might not look like the Christians you see on television or in your church, but are you following Jesus? The goal is to follow Him so closely that you begin to look more like Him every day, not cosmetically, but your character will be like His.

EVENING

- REFLECT -

Who do you follow? Why?

_____

_____

_____

Do you ever wonder if Jesus can provide for your every need? How have you seen His providing in the past?

_____

_____

_____

How do you identify with Peter in this text?

_____

_____

_____

How does it make you feel knowing if you follow Jesus, then He will make you into what He wants you to be?

_____

_____

_____

FAN:

an

enthusiastic

admirer.

DAY 16

- THINK -

Who are you? This is a question that is tremendously difficult to answer, and even to understand. When a person gets asked this question, he or she may answer it in terms of title, family, status, career, accomplishments or any other number of categories. Often times, when we find that our course in life seems to be off track, it comes as a result of having a skewed identity of ourselves. If we get caught up in thinking we're important because we're in step with every new trend, then our value comes from pop culture. If our worth comes from our athletic abilities, then our world gets shattered when we break a bone and have to sit on the bench. However, when we claim our identity from the true and pure source, it changes everything . . . for the best.

- FOCUS -

Start your day by reading Matthew 19:16-26.

As Jesus ministry advances, word spreads far and wide of his teaching and reputation. As a result, Jesus is approached by a young, wealthy man who is curious as to how he can obtain eternal life. Through the course of the discussion, the man becomes discouraged and frustrated. Whether he was looking for a pat on the back or a simple instruction is unclear. What is certain is that Jesus poses a challenge that seems more difficult to him than following the list of commands he's just been given: he is told to go sell all that he has and give it to the poor. Then, he may come and follow Jesus. The young man leaves Jesus' presence, saddened by Jesus' words.

- CONSIDER -

The young man showed an interest in gaining eternal life, but had trouble accepting the cost of following Jesus. Somehow, money had taken a place of importance in his life that Jesus wanted to have. The rich man still found some of his identity in wealth, and it became a roadblock between him and Jesus. Jesus wanted the rich man to follow him, but he also wanted the man to break away from the stronghold of money in his life.

Followers of Jesus find their identity in him. When we gain our identity from other sources, it undermines who we are and our devotion to Jesus. All human sources of identity are temporary. Only by finding value in being a son, daughter, follower of Jesus, can we truly have an eternal source of our identity. As we learn to reclaim our identity in Christ, we are able to remove many of the roadblocks that stand between us and following Jesus. As well, through developing a Christ-centered identity, we are also freed from pursuing performance-based value.

- APPLY -

Where is your source of identity? What is it that gives your life value and worth? Today, make it your goal to trace back the sources from which you find your identity. You may know right away, or it may take some time to figure out. Below are a few questions that may help you think. Before your evening reflection time, try to answer some of these questions and determine where your identity is currently coming from.

- What people/things make you feel really good or bad about yourself?
- Which of your titles do you like the most?
- What are the things (even good ones) that are the most diffi-

cult to surrender to follow Jesus?

- When you think about yourself, where/who did these thoughts originally come from?

EVENING

- REFLECT -

Being completely transparent, what are the sources of your identity?

_____

_____

_____

How much of the way you see yourself comes from Jesus? Others?

_____

_____

_____

How are worldly sources of identity getting in the way of you following Jesus?

_____

_____

_____

What do you think Jesus might want you to do to realign your identity with him?

_____

_____

_____

Consider one of the false sources of identity that you've allowed to shape you. Focus on this one. Pray and ask God to help you replace it with an identity found in Jesus. If a new picture of your identity comes to mind, take time to embrace it. Allow this new picture to saturate your mind and heart.

DAY 17

- THINK -

It has been said by some that a person's name is the most
beautiful word in their language. When someone addresses you
by name, they are placing value upon you. By using your name,
a person shows that they recognize you and, in a way, that they
know you. When someone knows and uses your name, it feels
good. When someone forgets your name, doesn't know it, or
mispronounces it, things get a little awkward. Just imagine
how bad it would be if someone decided to choose a name for
you that just didn't fit, and insisted on calling you by that name
for the rest of your life. That could be downright irritating and
painful.

- FOCUS -

Start your day by reading John 1:35-42.

This passage may seem familiar, as it covers the same event
that you read about on Day 1 of the journal. However, it takes
on new meaning today. After Jesus began gathering men to follow him, Simon and Andrew spent the day with Jesus. Around
early evening (the 10th hour, or 4:00 p.m.), Jesus makes a surprising statement to Simon. He tells him that he's being given a
new name: Peter. This is particularly strange, as the two haven't
known each other for very long.

- CONSIDER -

There are a few other people in the Bible who are given new names. Abram and Sarai become Abraham and Sarah after God promises to make them a great nation. Jacob (the deceiver) is renamed Israel (he struggles with God). Saul is renamed Paul once he moves from killing Christians to proclaiming Christ. Each name change is significant, drawing attention to a new phase of life in following God.

A name change can signify a break from the past. To be honest, some of us need to break away from a history that has miscategorized us. Names from the past can come back to haunt us. Many times, these names keep us prisoner to things we've walked through that Christ has asked us to leave behind.

Possibly you were abused and you took on the title "dirty." Perhaps you were ridiculed as a small kid and were labeled "loser." It could be that a parent constantly called you "not good enough." There could be a laundry list of names that you're carrying around like cumbersome weights.

The promise of a new name isn't just for a select few people who lived thousands of years ago. Revelation records a promise for those who remain faithful to Jesus. They'll be given a new name: a special name only known to the recipient and Jesus. While faithful followers can look forward to this moment, we don't have to wait that long to start leaving some old names behind.

- APPLY -

Scripture calls followers sons and daughters of God. However, many of you cling to other names that were not given to you by Him. Today, recognize all the incorrect names that you've taken on. They may be names given to you by others, ones you've assumed that people have given you, and names that Satan has twisted and distorted you into believing. As you pray about this for the day, ask for God to show you the false names you've let creep in to your life. Each time you recognize one, write it down. Pray and ask for God to replace it with a new name – based on His truth and His Word.

EVENING

- REFLECT -

What false names have you taken on?

_____

_____

_____

What are some replacement names you need to receive and believe?

_____

_____

_____

Read Revelation 2:17? What's your reaction to this verse?

_____

_____

_____

How would it change your life if you could live with only the names Jesus gives you?

_____

_____

_____

Make a commitment tonight to eliminate the false names you've been given and adopt the names Jesus gives you. Visualize how you can continue this practice every day. Pray and ask for God to help you with this process.

DAY 18

- THINK -

We have covered a lot of ground the past couple of weeks. This may feel a little overwhelming at times reading about what you have to give up, what you have to sacrifice, how you have to deny, die and follow. Maybe you were just hoping to believe in Jesus and the rest would take care of itself. There is some truth to that idea, but the Bible does remind us that true faith is accompanied by action. Even though you are in the process of changing your lifestyle to follow Jesus, you need to be reminded to also trust God and rest in who He says you are.

- FOCUS -

(Old Testament)

Read the following passages and write down who God says you are.

Genesis 3:19

_____

Genesis 4:11

_____

From these passages we can see how God says man was free, but man disobeyed and was therefore cursed.

Leviticus 20:26; Deuteronomy 7:6

These are a few passages God gives after giving the Ten Commandments. God is setting apart a people who will be part of his plan of salvation.

Deuteronomy 9:4-6

In the midst of our disobedience God is faithful. He was faithful to His word and faithful to us. God keeps his word and yet works on our behalf. That is a God who is worthy to be followed.

(New Testament)

1 Corinthians 3:1-4

All of us want to fit in somewhere. We want to follow the person who is the most popular and famous. Being concerned about what everyone else thinks and how we fit in causes us to be worldy.

1 Corinthians 3:5-9

The progression continues from the worldly to those who have had the gospel planted in their heart. It doesn't matter who plants the seed of the gospel. What matters is that it has been planted in the lives of others.

1 Corinthians 3:10-17

The Holy Spirit has been placed inside the heart of those who believe.

1 Corinthians 3:18-23

- APPLY -

If we are of Christ, then how should we live?

Matthew 5:13

Matthew 5:14

Matthew 10:26-31

John 15:5-8

John 15:9-17

Acts 3:24-26

Galatians 3:26-29

Galatians 4:4-7

EVENING

- REFLECT -

Just take time to thank God for letting you know who you are.

_____

_____

_____

_____

_____

_____

_____

_____

_____

_____

_____

_____

DAY 19

- THINK -

Today is day 19 in your Not a Fan journal. Think back to where you were when you first opened this book. Are you different now than you were before? Has your relationship with Jesus changed? Hopefully, the past few weeks have been an incredible journey of learning and living to follow Jesus. Truly seeing what a follower looks like can be a life-altering experience. In the days ahead, keep making it a priority to pursue your relationship with Jesus. After all, it's the heartbeat of Jesus for you to be a fully committed follower. A life of following Jesus involves a daily pursuit of Him. Today may be a good day to remember that in this journey, you're not alone.

- PAUSE -

Stop to give thanks to God for anything He's done in your life the past few weeks. Then, invite Him into your day today. Ask Him to open your eyes to His truth, and guide you in the journey to come.

- FOCUS -

Start your day by reading John 16:5-16.

The book of John records some of the final extended conversations Jesus has with his disciples. The passage you just read from John 16 is one such conversation. Jesus, intentional as always, has some important words to share with his followers.

This one concerns the Holy Spirit. Earlier, as recorded in John 14, Jesus introduces the Holy Spirit as another Helper. As you dig into the Greek word that's translated into English as "another," you find the word allos. Allos means "another of the same kind." In other words, Jesus was promising a helper like himself to his followers.

Jesus reveals a few important things in this passage. Jesus points out that it's good that He's going away so that the Holy Spirit could come. Why is this good? Because while Jesus spends time with His followers, the Holy Spirit will live INSIDE His followers. As well, the Holy Spirit is promised to come and convict the world of sin, guide believers into all truth and keep teaching them what the Father has to say.

- CONSIDER -

This may be one of the most powerful truths you will ever hear. The Holy Spirit is God living within you. The Holy Spirit is a gift from Jesus to those who surrender their lives to him. The Holy Spirit continues to teach God's truth to His people.

This is a near mind-bending thought. God lives inside His followers, teaching them and correcting them from the inside. This mysterious gift is one that cannot easily be explained. You can be sure the Holy Spirit is a powerful helper. He guides the believer. He reminds them of Jesus' truth. He is closer than a brother. He expresses the heartbeat of the father.

- APPLY -

God has given you a precious gift in the form of the Holy Spirit. Today, instead of asking yourself questions, meditate on this great mystery: The Holy Spirit lives within is followers. Pray and ask God to reveal more about Hthe Holy Spirit to you. Return to John 16 for periodic reminders.

EVENING

- REFLECT -

What have you learned about the Holy Spirit today?

_____

_____

_____

Do you think the Holy Spirit is living in you? Why or why not?

_____

_____

_____

Why did Jesus send the Holy Spirit to His people?

_____

_____

_____

What difference does the Holy Spirit currently make in your life? Does this need to change??

_____

_____

_____

Continue to consider the mystery of the Holy Spirit dwelling in Jesus Followers. Don't stop asking God to reveal more and more truth to you about this reality.

DAY 20

- THINK -

There's a viral video that's been floating around the internet of a woman who is vacuuming at a retail store. She's using the hose attachment, and is fervently sweeping her way across the carpeted floor. Even though she is diligently working and focused on the task at hand, she has failed to recognize that the hose has completely detached from the vaccum. This continues on for around three quarters of a minute before she realizes the problem. The moment she notices, she immediately walks over to the vaccum unit to reconnect the hose. Unfortunately, she wasn't fast enough to avoid being recorded on someone's camera phone and broadcast across the internet. Staying connected to the source means everything.

- FOCUS -

Start your day by reading John 5:19-23- 15:1-8.

Fair warining: there's some heavy duty material in these passages.

In John 5, Jesus reveals something essential to who He is and what He does: He imitates His Father. Jesus goes so far as to say that He can ONLY do what His father does. This is an amazing truth to realize. Jesus was dependent on His father.

Fast forward to John 15. Here, Jesus presents His disciples with a clear picture of the type of relationship His followers are to have with Him. He is the vine. His followers are the branches. God the Father is the gardener. It's a pretty simple picture, but powerful. When branches stay connected to the vine (or trunk), then water and nutrients can flow through them to produce fruit. When a branch is cut or ripped off of the vine, it begins to die immediately and can no longer produce fruit. Verse 8 shows that the Father receives glory when branches (his people) bear much fruit.

- CONSIDER -

Jesus had to stay connected with His Father in order to know what to do. Jesus tells His followers to stay connected to Him in order to lead fruit-producing lives. As you learned yesterday, when Jesus left, he provided the gift of the Holy Spirit to live inside of believers and connect them to the Father. The Holy Spirit continues to guide followers into all truth: the truth that comes from the Father

Taking Jesus' teaching to heart, the only way for a believer to produce fruit is to remain connected to the vine – to Jesus, and ultimately to the Father. And Christ-followers connect through the Holy Spirit. But how often do you stop to make sure that you're connected to the Father? How long do you keep vacuuming without realizing the hose has been disconnected?

One of the greatest challenges for a follower is to stay in step with the leading of the Holy Spirit, so that we can know and respond to the will of the Father.   A follower, by definition, follows. That means that a Jesus follower must be led by Jesus. Learning to recognize, listen, and respond to the voice of the Holy Spirit helps the believer to do just that.   And in order to produce any kind of fruit that pleases the Father, believers must remain connected.

- APPLY -

Carve out some time today to do a simple exercise. Find an electronic device (with no battery) that has a detachable power cord. This may work best if it's a device that produces light or sound. Plug in the device and turn it own. Pause to consider how the electricity flows from the outlet through the power cord into the device and produces a product. Now, re-read John 15:1-8. How does each part of this passage relate to your device. Now unplug it while the device is running. Note what happens. Read John 15:1-8 again. Examine where the breakdown is taking place in the device and how the same issue is addressed in the passage

EVENING

- REFLECT -

How do you feel, knowing that Jesus could only do what He saw His Father doing?

_____

_____

_____

What did you learn through the electronic device exercise today?

_____

_____

_____

How often do you find yourself checking to be sure you're still connected to the Holy Spirit? Trying to do things on your own?

_____

_____

_____

What would you have to do to align your life with the leading of the Holy Spirit? What kind of fruit might be waiting if you do?

_____

_____

_____

Put down this journal. Take time to talk to your Heavenly Father and ask for Him to help you walk in step with the Holy Spirit. Ask for Him to reveal more of his heart to you through the Holy Spirit. Then, be silent and give Him some space to speak to you.

DAY 21

- THINK -

If you ever want to learn a lot about patience and discipline, try planting a garden. First, you have to get ahold of some seeds. Then you've got to prepare the ground (or containers if you're an urban gardener). After that, you plant the seeds, lightly cover them with soil, and wait. Of course, you make sure they have plenty of water and sunlight. If weeds start to creep in, you carefully remove them without disturbing the seed. You may even fertilize the soil. For the most part, however, you do a lot of waiting. One day, the plant sprouts through the soil. Slowly and steadily, the plant grows bigger and bigger. If the plant is nurtured and protected just right, after many days or years, the plant will finally produce an ear of corn, a vine filled with cucumbers or a patch speckled with strawberries. There's little you can do to rush the process, but it's all worth the work if the harvest is good.

- FOCUS -

Start your day by reading John 15:9-17 & Luke 6:43-45.

The John 15 passage is a continuation of Jesus' discussion with his followers about the vine and branches. Here, Jesus once again emphasizes how necessary it is to stay connected to him in order to bear fruit. In fact, in verse 16, Jesus reveals that He chose His followers for the purpose of bearing lasting fruit. Jesus' followers weren't just chosen so He could have a wide friend base or become bodyguards when angry Jewish leaders came around. They were chosen to bear fruit. In Luke 6, Jesus explains that good trees go on to bear good fruit, while bad trees cannot. Likewise, if fruit from a tree is examined, it will become obvious whether the tree is good or bad.

Even from chapter 1 of Genesis, the concept of bearing fruit is introduced (Genesis 1:11-12). God designed plants to produce fruit of it's own kind. Throughout the gospels, especially Matthew, this theme comes up over and over again. As such, a follower must pay attention to this repeated analogy.

- INVESTIGATE -

Every day, you have the potential to produce fruit. But what is fruit? In a plant fruit is the result of the time, energy and growth of the plant. The end result of a pumpkin seed is a pumpkin. In a believer, the fruit is the outcome of a life that remains connected to Jesus. Some fruit that is produced is on the inside (a heart of gratitude, faith, joy, etc.) and other fruit is produced externally (making disciples, worship, living in step with the Holy Spirit, etc.).

Look up the following passages to learn more about what the fruit of a Jesus follower looks like. As you read, keep one thing in mind. You cannot produce fruit on your own. Fruit is the result of remaining connected to God through the Holy Spirit and of allowing Him to work in your life.

Galatians 5:22-26
Ephesians 5:8-11
Hebrews 13:15

- APPLY -

Take a bold step today and ask a few people what kind of fruit (reword the question if you need to) you are producing. Give them permission to give you honest feedback. Listen to what they say, and try not to get upset if you don't like the answer.

After talking to them, take time to assess yourself honestly. What kind of fruit are you producing? What fruit is missing?

EVENING

- REFLECT -

In your research earlier, what examples of fruit did you come across?

_____

_____

_____

What did other people have to say about the kind of fruit being produced in your life? What do you see in yourself?

_____

_____

_____

Genesis 1:11-12 says that plants are designed to bear fruits containing seeds according to it's own kind. The same is true for you. In other words, you reproduce who/what you are. As you currently are, what kind of fruit will come the seeds you produce?

_____

_____

_____

Are there steps you need to take in order to stay connected to Jesus? If so, what are they?

_____

_____

_____

Think back through the gardening analogy from the start of today. Remember that the plant's job is to develop roots, soak up water and nutrients, and develop. Picture the ways that you can connect yourself to Jesus and grow in Him. If need be, confess to Him the places where you're trying to bear fruit from your own strength. Rest at peace in your relationship with Him tonight.

DAY 22

- THINK -

There are many people in the world today who are directionally challenged. They simply cannot tell which way is north, south, east or west. Just for fun take a minute and point which way you think is north. If you have a way of checking this, see how accurate you are. People who struggle with directions always speak in terms of landmarks.

If you struggle with directions it's a good idea to get a GPS. The voice guided turn by turn is a lifesaver for those people who don't know which way is north or east. However, GPS systems are pointless if you don't listen to what the device says. When you miss a turn you will hear the unit saying, "when possible make a legal U-turn" over and over again.

Some of us are just bad at following directions, while others of us get distracted. We start looking at the scenery, crowds, lights, or zoned out and next thing we know we have missed our turn. Life can be similar in that we may know where we want to end up, but not sure how to get there. We know we want to follow Jesus, but don't really know how to do that. Usually it's because we are directionally challenged or we just don't pay attention.

- FOCUS -

Start your day be reading Mark 1: 29-38. What possible rut do you see Jesus returning to every day in this text?

In Mark 1 we find Jesus has just healed a Peter's mother in law, then freed several people of sickness and from demon posses-sion. The text says the entire town was there to see Jesus. This went on well into the night.

Can you imagine the excitement of the disciples? These were ordinary guys who were now following Jesus as his inner posse. They had it made and were probably excited to be part of the Jesus train. When the disciples find him to let him know every-one was looking for Him. Jesus says, "Let's go somewhere else so I can preach, for this is why I have come."

The disciples are thinking, "Are you kidding me Jesus? Why would you leave? You are successful here. You are popular here! People are coming to you in droves to see you. It doesn't make sense to leave. Let's stay here and enjoy it." The ideas of success and popularity were something the disciples had never experienced before and it was becoming a distraction.

Jesus got up early and went out to pray. He had just stayed up late the night before and then got up early the next day to spend time with His heavenly father. He didn't say he was too tired because He knew how important it was for Him to have God reveal to Him his mission for the day. In the midst of all the excitement, Jesus remained focused on the mission God had given Him to preach the good news.

- CONSIDER -

Read through the following passages and see how many of these men made it a practice to pray in the morning. Praying in the morning is more than just telling the Father in Heaven good morning, but it is getting our directions for the day. What you will find is the more you pray, the more time you spend listening to God rather than talking.

Abraham got up very early to stand before the Lord (Genesis 19:27).

Jacob woke up with the first light of the morning to worship God after having seen a vision of angels in the night (Genesis 28:18).

Moses went early to meet the Lord at Sinai (Exodus 34:4).

Joshua got an early start when he prepared to capture Jericho (Joshua 6:12).

Gideon made his way at dawn to examine the fleece he had placed on the ground to discern God's will (Judges 6:38).

Job left his bed at an early hour to offer sacrifices to the Lord in behalf of his children. (Job 1:5)

- APPLY -

For the next seven days get up 15 minutes early to spend time in prayer. Ask the Lord to refocus your life and give you directions for the day. Spend at least five of those minutes listening. You may not hear a thing, but you may hear the voice of the One you follow.

- REFLECT -

How do you know what to do every day?

_____

_____

_____

If you were to start every day off with prayer and only do what you were told to do from God would you be able to do it? Would you be more concerned that you wouldn't hear or that you wouldn't follow?

_____

_____

_____

How much of your prayers are listening? Why do you think it is this way?

_____

_____

_____

When it comes to following Jesus why is it so important to pray?

_____

_____

_____

DAY 23

- THINK -

Being a parent is arguably one of the toughest jobs in the world. From midnight bottles to soccer games and doctoring wounds to preparing meals, parents invest a lot for the benefit of their kids. Occasionally, kids decide to give something back to mom and dad. There's the surprise breakfast-in-bed delivery of half-spilled orange juice and soggy cereal. Handmade hearts and crayon scribbled notes and coupon books are just a few of the gifts that children use to express their love and win the heart of mom and dad. And these gifts are loved and valued and treasured, but the truth is there is a far greater and rarer gift that blesses parents: simple obedience. Sure, obedience doesn't sound overly glamorous, but it can be the greatest expression of love that a child can give.

- EXPLORE -

Obedience is a command and a characteristic of fully com-mitted followers. When it comes to the heart of the Heavenly Father, it's clear that obedience is even better than sacrifices (1 Samuel 15:22). Scripture reveals much more about what God has to say about obedience. Today, your challenge is to unearth some of these truths.

Spend time today exploring the Bible to see what God has to say about the relationship between followers and believers. You won't be given any specific verses to study, so you'll have to take some initiative to seek out passages that talk about obedi-ence. Below are a few suggestions of how you might go about finding them

- Read through the book of John. Make notes of places where Jesus modeled obedience or addressed obedience.
- Look up the word "obey" in a concordance (you can find one in the back of your bible or online). Read through several verses that talk about obedience and summarize them.
- Pick a few chapters from one of the gospels (Matthew, Mark, Luke or John). Read through them, taking notes of the commands or instructions given by Jesus. Consider how important obedience is to Jesus.

EVENING

As you explored earlier today, what did you learn about obedience?

_____

_____

_____

Read John 14:15, 14:23, 15:10 and 1 John 2:5? What common theme do you find?

_____

_____

_____

According to these verses, is it possible to love God and be disobedient?

_____

_____

_____

If you really took these verses seriously, do you think you would live a more obedient life? Why or why not?

_____

_____

_____

Even Jesus had to remain connected to His Father to be obedient. Pray and ask for God's help as you seek to live a life of obedience. Examine your heart to see if there is any disobedience that you need to confess and repent of. Spend time in your Father's presence, letting him hear your heart and listening to his voice.

DAY 24

- THINK -

Let's be honest - it's not really too hard to figure out what's important to people. Find a fellow student on the weekend and see what they do regularly. Ask someone what he looks forward to doing. Check the hours logged on your friend's game console. Take a quick glance over your friend's twitter feed or Facebook timeline. Listen to the conversation topics that keep repeating in your classroom. Chances are, you won't have to put too much effort in hunting before you have a good idea what someone is about. Should it come as a surprise that the same is true for you too? Regardless of what you might try and convince people is true, the people you're closest to don't even have to guess at what tops the chart of your priorities. What you're passionate about shines through.

- FOCUS -

Start your day by reading Mark 12:28-34.

As recorded in the gospels, many times Jesus takes a question and answers it in a way that's more riddle than direct response. This passage, however, is not one such example. When Jesus is asked by one of the teachers in the law about the greatest command, there is no hesitation. There is no riddle. There is no analogy. Jesus points out to the man that the pinnacle of all commands is to love God with all one's heart, soul, mind and strength. As and added bonus, Jesus throws in the second greatest commandment, "Love your neighbor as yourself." Jesus and the teacher continue on briefly, in agreement over these truths. The conversation closes with Jesus' affirmation of the man's nearness to God's Kingdom. Apparently, this transaction was enough to hush any bystanders.

Both Jesus and the teacher of the law would have known that this was not a new concept. In fact, this particular command can be found in Deuteronomy 6:5. Deuteronomy, being one of the first 5 books of the Jewish, Hebrew Bible (also known as the Torah). The Torah would have been completely memorized by traditional Jewish boys by the age of 12. The Torah contains a total of 613 commands. Out of all of these commands, Jesus selects one as most important. And this one command puts God the Father right in the middle of a follower's life.

- CONSIDER -

Loving God with all one's heart, soul, mind and strength could be simply summed up as worship. Unfortunately, modern culture considers worship to be singing songs to God. Worship is so much bigger than this. Worship is putting God first in one's life and increasing God's value in a person's own eyes and the eyes of others. Worship is thanking God for a sunset. Worship is sharing the truth of Jesus with a friend. Worship is prioritizing God over everything else in a believer's life.

Most likely, you understand how difficult it is to live out this command in this day and age. Your heart is attracted and devoted to a thousand different things. Your soul gets fed by the wrong sources. Your mind is bombarded with information and images. Your strength is depleted by your daily activities list. Even though Jesus is clear that this is the most important command, are you really living it out in your everyday life? A true follower of Jesus is a worshipper, and not just on Sundays.

- APPLY -

Hit the reset button today. Write this verse down and carry it with you for the day. Every time you think about it, pull the verse out and read it. Then, stop to pray for the Holy Spirit's help in living it out. As things pop up throughout the day, consider what you can do to move other things out of the way and move Jesus into the center. Find out what things have really been the priority in your heart, soul, mind and strength. Make a commitment for God to take their place, even if it comes at a cost.

<u>EVENING</u>

- REFLECT -

How are you doing at loving God with ALL your
- · Heart?
- · Soul?
- · Mind?
- · Strength?

What are the things that get more of your time than your relationship with God?

Is this command too radical to live out in the twenty-first century? Why or why not?

_____

_____

_____

How can you be more intentional about worshipping God in your life?

_____

_____

_____

Tonight, don't ask God for anything. Make it a priority for the rest of the day to take every opportunity to worship God, praise Him, thank Him. Find as many excuses as you can to focus on who God is and what He has done. Let Him receive your attention and appreciation for the rest of the day.

DAY 25

- THINK -

If you turn on your television or computer for more than five minutes, chances are, you'll start getting bombarded by ads. Television commercials appeal to your ego and desires. They try to convince you that their product will make you happy. Customized advertisements pop up on your e-mail and social media pages when you're on the web. The radio draws your attention to even more things that your life will be incomplete without. Every product is designed to put you in the middle, and sway you that you'll have a more fulfilled life if you buy in. If you decided to base your life choices on these types of media, you'd wind up being pretty self-centered and very greedy.

- FOCUS -

Start your day by reading John 13:1-17

Here are a few highlights of what is taking place in this passage:

- Jesus is in Jerusalem. He knows that His death is almost here, and is already aware that Judas will betray him.
- Typically, the role of washing a person's feet was the job of the servant; this job was reserved for the least-honored person.
- Jesus takes off His outer robe and washes the feet of all the disciples who are gathered, even Judas'.
- Jesus instructs his followers to follow the example that He has set.

As you read the Bible, you discover that Jesus was alive long before He came down to earth as a baby boy. He was present even at the point of creation, and he lived in companionship with His Father. Even so, Jesus gives that all up to restore the relationship of mankind to the Father. One moment, Jesus is living in the perfect glory of His Father. The next moment, He's on the Earth, surrounded by pain and rejection. And He chose to wash the feet of His followers. If anybody in the universe had the right to opt out of washing dirt and donkey droppings off the feet of people, it was Jesus. But Jesus sacrificed comfort and glory and perfection for the sake of serving His people.

Jesus set the ultimate example of service. He took himself out of the center and made sure that his father got the rightful place of honor. He allowed Himself to be made nothing so that other's had a clear path to see His Father.

Jesus called His followers to do the same. By serving others in Jesus' name, His followers reflect the heart of Jesus and break down the barriers of pride that often get in the way of a person's journey toward Jesus. Living a life of service is more than planning an afternoon yard raking or a short-term mission trip. Serving others means being ready to meet needs that pop up in everyday life on the spot.

- APPLY -

Find a creative way to serve someone today. Don't pre-plan anything. Just prayerfully look for needs throughout your day. When an opportunity arises, do your best to meet that need (or start the process of meeting that need). As you serve, whether a big or small act, make sure to serve in the name of Jesus. The Bible instructs us to give a gift as small as a cup of cold water in Jesus' name. Serve someone today and point them toward

Jesus in the process.

EVENING

- REFLECT -

How were you able to serve today?

_____

_____

_____

As you looked for opportunities to serve, what was going on in your heart?

_____

_____

_____

What are some of the needs you noticed today that you hadn't seen before?

_____

_____

_____

Why do you think Jesus took the time in His last hours to wash His disciples' feet?

_____

_____

_____

Go back and re-read Philippians 2:5-11. Meditate on this passage for the rest of the day. Pray through how you might be able to better imitate Jesus's attitude in your everyday life.

DAY 26

- THINK -

Over the past two days we have read about worship and serving. We know from Romans 12:1-2 that worship and serving go hand-in-hand. The truth is, when we serve others, we are actually worshipping God. Fans of Jesus often talk about worship, but rarely follow through. Worship/serving is part of a follower's life.

- FOCUS -

Read Psalm 100.

In the book of Psalms, David—who was known as a man after God's own heart--uses the word "worship", which can also be translated as "serve" when examining the original language. Worship and serve are interchangeable in this text.

Worship is often defined as our response to God for who He is and what He has done. David does a great job explaining in this text who God is and why God has done what He has done.

- CONSIDER -

God is God!

This might not seem like a big deal or something new, but this should come as good news.   Look at the people around you— your friend, family, etc. Aren't you glad THEY aren't God? Even your best friends may be great companions, but they would be terrible and being God. They'd forget to answer your prayers—

after all, sometimes they forget to respond to text messages! And spending eternity with them, when all you can handle is a few hours before needing your space? There isn't a person who could substitute for God.

Your friends,
Your parents,
Your teachers,
Your favorite athlete or movie star…
They are not God.

For some of you this is a big deal. You have been told most of your life you are worthless, will amount to nothing, you aren't good enough, or that you have to be something you aren't.

Good friends, parents, teachers, will all point you to the One true God who defines who you are, and who doesn't change or waiver. You know exactly who He is and who you are to be.

You belong to God!

Have you ever put together a puzzle, built a sandcastle, or made something out of Legos with kids? What is the first thing they want to do after completion? Destroy it. And we get mad and frustrated with them. But then we remember it is theirs…they made it and they can do with it what they want.

It is God who made us and we are His. He can do with us what he wants. He made us and we belong to Him. The reason we often get mad at God is because we start to think we deserve something from Him. "God, how could you let me get sick? God how could you allow abuse to happen? God, how could you…," and we shake our fist, but we forget that He does not have to give us anything (not even our next breath). We have done nothing for Him…we do not deserve anything, but He continues to give.

God is good!

God could destroy us because He is God, but he does not because He is good. He is faithful to us and He loves us. He longs to have a relationship with us and sent His own son as an act of love in order to rescue us from our sin, from this world, and from death. All that we have is from Him because He is good. He is worthy to be praised, worshiped and followed.

- APPLY -

The application is simple. Spend some time today set apart to praise God because of who He is and what He has done. Thank Him for sending His son as an example for us to follow. Then serve the Lord by serving others.

EVENING

- REFLECT -

Why are you thankful God is God?

_____

_____

_____

How does it make you feel knowing you belong to God?

_____

_____

_____

_____

In what ways have you seen God as good?

_____

_____

_____

Knowing who God is, how will you respond?

_____

_____

_____

DAY 27

- THINK -

Derek is a man with a photographic memory. He remembers everything that he reads. If you were to ask him how his mind works, he would tell you that the inside of his brain looks like a series of filing cabinets. Any time he wants to remember something, he just has to mentally find the right filing cabinet, open up the proper drawer, and pull the file out to read it. Over the course of time, Derek has filled his filing cabinets will all kinds of information: some useful, some ridiculous. Recently, Derek dedicated two years to studying through every passage of scripture in the Bible. Whenever he wants, Derek can recall God's Word to his mind. But he doesn't just stop because he's got it all filed away. He continues to spend time in scripture, getting to know the Bible and its author even better.

- FOCUS -

Start your day by reading Matthew 4:1-11.

After His baptism, Jesus obeys the leading of the Spirit by going out into the wilderness. Instead of storming Jerusalem to signify the start of His ministry, Jesus goes in the opposite direction. He leaves behind the crowds and goes to a place of solitude to be with his Father. During this time, he spends forty days in a fast (not eating any food). Now Jesus is hungry. And Satan uses this moment to exploit Jesus' weakness. Satan begins with a plot to exploit Jesus' power by trying to entice him to turn the nearby rocks into bread. As hungry as He was, Jesus was focused on his Father's will even more. Jesus' response is both from and about scripture. In no uncertain terms, Jesus quotes from Deuteronomy to remind Satan that man is fueled by more than just food, but by the words of God. Two more times, the devil tries to tempt Jesus. Both times, Jesus responds by quoting Old Testament passages. After this, Satan leaves.

- CONSIDER -

Jesus, after fasting forty days, was ready for battle. Sure, his stomach was empty, but his mind and heart were filled with the words of his Father. During his time in the wilderness, Jesus fasted and prayed. But no doubt, he also spent time thinking about scripture. When temptation came along, Jesus was well equipped to combat the lies of Satan with the truth of God's word (a feat failed by men ever since Adam and Eve). Jesus didn't fall back on his own wisdom or clever responses. He went directly to Scripture to expose Satan's faulty logic, and defeat Satan's attempt to cause Jesus to give in to temptation.

- APPLY -

To prepare for his ministry, Jesus obediently followed the Spirit into the wilderness to fast and spend time with His Father. Today is a great day to fast from something in order to give God more time and focus. Choose something that would normally be a part of your day and sacrifice it for the sake of time with Jesus. You may choose to give up food, television, music, playing basketball, or any number of other things. Take the time that you would have spent with those other things and dive into scripture instead. Get to know the words and heart of God better. Commit some scripture to memory. Allow your fast to be a sacrifice to God and dedicate your time to focusing on Him.

EVENING

What did you fast from today and how did things go?

_____

_____

_____

Did making a sacrifice help you to focus? Explain?

_____

_____

_____

What place does the Word of God have in your daily life?

_____

_____

_____

When was the last time that you intentionally spent time memorizing scripture? Are you satisfied with that answer?

_____

_____

_____

Where do you think God would bring victory to your life if you stored away scripture in your heart and mind?

_____

_____

_____

List the ways that you can bring scripture into more areas of your life. Consider how fasting from something on a regular basis might clear up space for Jesus and the Word to occupy. As you pray about this, ask God to draw your heart closer to his Word.

_____

_____

_____

_____

_____

_____

_____

_____

_____

_____

_____

DAY 28

- THINK -

One of the best parts about a dating relationship or a healthy marriage is intentionality. By being intentional, a guy plans out a fun date night or writes down some tender words to express his feelings. A young lady takes time to thoughtfully select a gift that she knows her boyfriend will like. A husband and wife go out of their way to create space to be together, express their love, and to be flexible when the other has something big going on. These relationships don't just start and end when the couple is spending time together. They think about one another, find ways to sneak in extra communication with each other, and invest time into the relationship, even when they're apart. Without being intentional, the relationship would be a mess. Intentionality is the driving force behind a growing relationship.

- FOCUS -

Start your day by reading Luke 19:1-10.

By this point in His ministry, Jesus has been teaching and healing throughout Galilee and Judea. He's moving steadily toward Jerusalem, where He will be crucified. On the way, Jesus passes through Jericho where he encounters Zacchaeus. Zacchaeus has a bad reputation for being a tax collector and for cheating people out of money. He's acquired some wealth along the way. As Jesus approaches, Zacchaeus climbs up in a tree to catch a glimpse of him. Jesus calls Zacchaeus out of the tree and declares that he'll be spending the day with Zacchaeus at his house. The crowd was disturbed at Jesus' choice for companionship. Zacchaeus, however, seized the opportunity to repent and repay those he had cheated. Jesus notes Zacchaeus' change of heart, and affirms that salvation has reached Zacchaeus' house.

- CONSIDER -

Jesus intentionally seized the opportunity to build a relationship with Zacchaeus. Whether he miraculously knew who Zacchaeus was or had met him previously is unknown. What is important is that Jesus took note of Zacchaeus and reached out to him.

Throughout the gospels, Jesus is intentionally taking steps to build, grow, and capitalize on relationships. Jesus chose to live life in relationship with the people around Him. He surrounded himself with disciples and apostles. He reached out to people who were hurting and seeking. Jesus was the living, breathing model of investing intentionally in relationships. Many of these relationships, like Zacchaeus', yielded the fruit of salvation.

Jesus didn't just build relationships for his own benefit; Jesus built relationships to show followers how to live life. How does your heart line up with Jesus' when it comes to building relationships with other people for the sake of the Kingdom? Are you looking for people in your world who need to hear the message of Jesus? Who you can have accountability with? Who you can do Kingdom work alongside?

- APPLY -

Walk through today with your eyes wide open. Prayerfully search for the people in your world who you need to be intentional with in relationship building. This may be someone who can spur you on in your walk with Jesus. It could be a person you know is hurting and needs the hope of Christ. This might be someone you feel like the Holy Spirit is leading you toward, even if you don't know why. Ask God to reveal a few people that you will intentionally build a relationship with in the next few months. With at least one of them, take a step toward building that relationship today.

EVENING

- REFLECT -

As you went throughout your day today, how did you see people differently?

Who did you encounter that you need to build a relationship with?

What steps will you take to reach out to this person? To invest in the relationship?

How difficult is it for you to be intentional in building purposeful relationships?

_____

_____

_____

Continue praying for God to reveal people in your life that you can build relationships with. Ask for the Holy Spirit to guide you in these relationships. As you grow in these relationships, remember to love others as you love yourself.

DAY 29

- THINK -

Several years ago there was a Nike commercial with Michael Jordan. For those who may not know, Michael Jordan is considered the greatest basketball player of all time. He won six NBA championships with the Chicago Bulls as well as one college national championship with the University of North Carolina. In this commercial Michael is talking about failure. He mentions how many shots he missed in his career, how many games he lost, and how many times he was trusted with the last second shot to win a game and missed. He finishes the commercial with the quote, "I have failed over and over and over again in my life. And that is why I succeed."

- FOCUS -

Read John 13:31-38; 18:15-18, 25-27

It's the night before Jesus' arrest and crucifixion, and Jesus is sitting with His disciples. Jesus takes the opportunity to give His "goodbyes" while they are all together. He tells them about His soon departure and informs them that they will not be able to go with Him. This would have been devastating news for the disciples who had left everything to follow Jesus.

Imagine as Jesus invites all of the disciples into a room. Jesus takes a towel, walks around the room, and washes all of the disciples feet—which He had never done before. The disciples had to wonder what was going on. He then tells that one of them is going to betray Him. As they are all looking round the room trying to figure out who it is, Peter speaks up. In that moment,

Peter must have felt like the relationship was ending, like he was being dumped. "You are my life, I have given up everything for you," he says.

Jesus replies, "Will you really lay down your life for me? Very truly I tell you, before the rooster crows, you will disown me three times!"

Can you imagine how Peter felt when he heard the rooster crow? Most likely, he felt like a failure.

- CONSIDER -

Reading on in the story, we learn that Jesus' words are true, and Peter does fail Him by denying that he knows Christ 3 times. This failure was so epic that it has been remembered and talked about for nearly 2000 years. This failure to follow would rival those failures of Adam and Eve in the garden, Moses in the desert, and David and Bathsheba. Although these failures have been written about and talked about for years, does that mean they are all that much different than our failure to follow Jesus?

You may not often think about the times you decide NOT to follow Jesus...the times we give into sin, the times we choose to be selfish, the times we gossip, the times we have moral failures, and the times we are ashamed to stand up for Jesus. And while our failures aren't recorded in the most popular book of all time, our failure to follow is no different than Peter's failure that night.

- APPLY -

Society today is pretty brutal when a celebrity fails. Their picture is plastered all over the news, if a trial is necessary it is broadcasted on television; and depending on the crime, their career may be over. We often wonder if they will ever be able to recover. Sometimes, the church can be just as brutal. Many times, when a follower of Jesus fails, the result is rejection, shame, and guilt, which is difficult to overcome.

Reading from Peter's life, he too could have said, "I have failed over and over and over again in my life. And that is why I succeed." Our failures are often part of our preparation. Peter did fail this time, but history tells us that Peter goes on to be one of the greatest missionaries that ever lived.

Today, you have to ask yourself these questions:

1. How have I failed to follow Jesus?
2. Who did my failure affect?
3. Am I dwelling on my failures, or choosing to see them how God sees them?

EVENING

- REFLECT -

When you fail, is it easy for you to try again? Or do you dwell on your mistakes?

_____

_____

_____

What's the most difficult part in facing others if you have failed them?

_____

_____

_____

How do you think Peter felt after he heard the rooster crow?

_____

_____

_____

Why do you think Peter was able to boldly proclaim the good news of Jesus throughout the rest of the New Testament?

_____

_____

_____

Are there people in your life who have failed you, but you have not forgiven them?

_____

_____

_____

Do you feel like you have failed God? Who could you share this with and how can you get back to following Jesus completely?

_____

_____

_____

DAY 30

- THINK -

Warning labels on medications are one of the most frightening pieces of material you will ever read. Many times the warning label sounds worse than the current ailment. There is a popular drug used for acne, which is known to potentially cause liver damage, joint pain, aggression, depression, and mental health disorders. Seems like quite the risk to take in order to clear up some blemishes. What is amazing is that these warnings are given to each person when they receive their prescription and they still take it. Seems like most people aren't reading the fine print, but desiring the benefits.

Several times in the gospels Jesus clearly puts a warning label out there. He wants everyone to know exactly what it is they are signing up for. Yes there are many benefits to following Jesus, but it does not come without a cost.

- FOCUS -

Read John 21:15-25. Write a warning label for what takes place in this text

_____

_____

_____

This is the first interaction Peter has had with Jesus following his denial of Jesus on the night of Jesus crucifixion. Three times Peter denied Jesus and three times Jesus asked Peter if he loved Him. What Jesus was doing here was reinstating Peter to his calling. The question "Do you love me?" is an appropriate question because we know we are willing to make sacrifices for what we love.

What is interesting is the first question Jesus asks Peter is the same question, but has a bit of a twist. He asks Peter if he loves him "more than these." Some would say Jesus is pointing at the other disciples, but that wouldn't really make sense considering Jesus was often correcting their arguments on who was the greatest. But what really brings the text to life is if Jesus is pointing at the large amount of fish they had just caught again because of the power of Jesus. 153 fish is great for a day of fishing and would have provided plenty of money for Peter and crew. Jesus is asking Peter if he loves him more than the comforts of this life. Peter do you love me more than the benefits you receive from me? Will you follow me even if these things aren't here? Will you stand up for me when everyone falls? Do you love me more than these?

Peter was hurt the last time Jesus asked because it was painfully obvious why Jesus was asking him this question three times. Three times Peter responded "Yes." Then Jesus followed by telling Peter to feed His sheep. Then Jesus tells Peter the type of death he was going to die. This death was going to be very similar to the death of Jesus. Then Jesus says "Follow me!"

I'm sure Peter had a fan moment. "I really like you Jesus and I like your teachings and I like the promise of eternal life, and I like the gifts you give, but I am not sure about following you so far as it costing my life." So he asks about everyone else. What will happen to the other disciples? Will they have to die like me or will their life be unaffected? Jesus says you don't worry about everyone else, but you follow me!

- CONSIDER -

Fans usually make their decisions based on what everyone around them is doing. If the crowd stands, then they stand, if the crowd moves, then they move, if the crowd sits, they sit, if the crowd is shouting, then they shout. You get the picture. The same is true with fans of Jesus. They do what everyone else is doing and going with the flow is the easiest thing to do, but when life gets difficult and you have to go against the flow, when you have to stand alone, what will you do?

Will you look at your comforts, and then back at Jesus? Will you look at your friends, and then back at Jesus? Will you look at your life and then back at Jesus? You have to choose. The Bible says in Joshua 24 it may be undesirable to serve the Lord, but we have to choose today whom we will serve. You have to choose if you are a fan or a follower.

- APPLY -

Followers of Jesus take what is known in scripture as the narrow road or the road less traveled. Jesus taught us a few examples of taking the road less traveled in John 21.

- He loved people more than comforts.
- He forgave someone who wronged him.
- He encouraged someone who failed to get back up and follow.

How can you do each of these today?

Now go and do these things or in the words of Jesus, "Feed my Sheep."

EVENING

- REFLECT -

What is the most frightening warning label you have read? If it would make you better to take the medicine, would you take it?

_____

_____

_____

What warning was Jesus giving Peter in John 21? What did Jesus expect Peter to do?

_____

_____

_____

What area of your life is keeping you from being a completely committed follower?

_____

_____

_____

How do you identify with Peter in this story today?